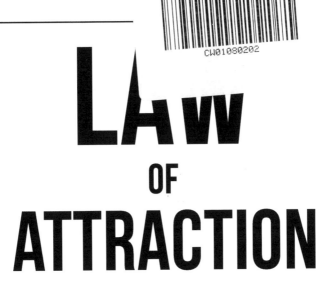

LAW
OF
ATTRACTION

Unleash the Power and Be The Creator of Your Life

*Law of Attraction Secrets
to Manifesting More Money,
More Power, More Love*

SIMON GRAY

FREE BONUS:
"Law of Attraction 30 Day Journal" Did you get it? If not, please do before moving forward.

CONTENTS

FREE BONUS HERE

When I first committed to understanding the Law of Attraction, I used this exact journal daily... and it
TRANSFORMED MY LIFE.

As a way to *thank you* for investing in yourself with this book...

I pass my 30 Day Law of Attraction Journal on to you... for *FREE*.

I do ask just one thing...Use it.

DOWNLOAD HERE FOR FREE - 30 Day

Journal: http://secretsofthelaw.com/

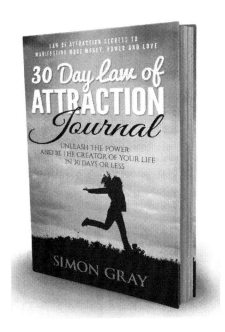

CHAPTER ONE

THE UNIVERSE IS LISTENING

All of life is energy.

The western world woke up to the realization that all of life is energy ever since Albert Einstein published the equation that rocked our world: E = MC2.

But what does it mean? It means that all of life — every quark, atom and molecule, every blade of grass, mote of dust and ray of the sun — is made up of *energy*. And of course, it means that we are made up energy, too. And while the Universe is ever-expanding, we are an expression of the dynamic, creative, extraordinary power of the Universe to create and expand itself.

The Law of Attraction is the magnetic property that enables this creation. For us humans, it means that the Law of Attraction is responding to the thoughts, words, feelings and actions that we hold and express every moment of our lives.

The Law of Attraction is working all the time. You don't have to command it, attract it, conquer it or get good at using it. The Law of Attraction is the property that propels how the stars are born, determines what you do for a living, and decides where you were born. It's what sets the tides, powers asteroids and fuels earthquakes. The Law of Attraction is behind everything that you experience, pleasant or unpleasant, joyous or horrendous. It is always in play.

The Law of Attraction is an equal-opportunity principle. It does not judge what you think or imagine or do, it gives equal weight to whatever you put out in the world. As Henry Ford said, "Whether you think you can or you think you can't: You're right." Whether you are spending time thinking about what you want or what you don't want, your thoughts ping the universe to attract more of what you are thinking about. And all things that happen to you come in response to these pings, in response to the vibrational invitation that you project. All of the people in your life, all of the chapters of your career and jobs, all of the good health or bad health that you experience are out-picturings of the thoughts that you have held at one time or another.

As you recognize the role and power of the Law of Attraction, your reality will shift because you will discover how powerful YOU are. You'll come to know your very thoughts as energy: energy that can be focused, clarified and molded into things, experiences and events. YOU can choose to manifest what you want in life — in relationships, your bank account, your work experience, your health, or whatever arena you choose — and find the happiness and fulfillment that you seek.

But the Law of Attraction is not just another feel-good exercise to fix your life or your circumstances. By working with it, you will likely find yourself transformed. As your circumstances improve, as you tap into your innate power to generate what you want in life, and as you discover how to play with this power, you will very likely be changed by it.

Working with the Law of Attraction is a spiritual journey that, if you stick with it, can lead you to a deeper connection with your own Spirit and with the laws of the Universe.

This book is a journey for you to discover the tremendous capacity you have within you to harness the Law of Attraction so that you can be happier, healthier and more fulfilled. How you can achieve your goals and have fun along the way. How your heart can be filled with the love you desire, how your body can relax in a stable and comfortable life, and how your spirit can express its truest, highest calling. By participating whole-heartedly in the Law of Attraction, you will discover many of the secrets of the Universe within yourself.

CHAPTER TWO

WHY POSITIVE THINKING DOESN'T WORK

Every day in every way I am getting better and better

Mind over matter is moot. Affirmations are all washed up. While the promise of positive thinking has been around for a long time, it just doesn't deliver.

But it sure is an integral part of popular culture these days. "Think positive." "Act as if." "You can do it." Discussions of positive thinking can be traced all the way back to the early 1800s when there was a flurry of writings about the power of the mind and of keeping an affirmative attitude. In his essays, Ralph Waldo Emerson promoted the importance of self-reliance and reasoned that our perception of reality can alter our reality. Ernest Holmes, founder of the Science of Mind movement, wrote several books about the power of the mind and stated very plainly: "thoughts are things." By 1898, Success Magazine was launched by Orison

Swett Marden and became one of the most popular and influential magazines in American history.

Philosophers threw their hat in the ring along with the others. The great William James said: "The greatest discovery of my generation is that man can alter his life simply by altering his attitude of mind." Not long after that, a pharmacist by the name of Émile Coué, studied hypnotism and autosuggestion in his spare time and told his patients to repeat a certain affirmation several times a day: *Every day in every way I am getting better and better.* This simple sentence is considered to be one of the first positive-thinking mantras or affirmations.

Perhaps the best-known author of positive-thinking wisdom is Napoleon Hill, whose book *Think and Grow Rich,* first published in 1937, has become one of the most successful books of all time. Hill lays down several effective tools to help you succeed in life, based on positive-thinking principles. His formula includes discussions about clarity of vision, working with others, how to handle defeat, healthy habits, and of course, keeping a positive mental attitude. He describes the benefit of working with others to generate the vision and energy towards that goal, and discusses other attitudes and actions that can propel the process. Of all of these directives, the one that has seen the greatest result, according to professional motivational speakers who work with them frequently, is to 'know very clearly where you want to go.'

These assertions of the power of the mind are inspiring, uplifting and very often helpful, but they fall short of really performing the miracles so many of us seek! After all, if having what you want in life is as simple as thinking positively, then a lot more people would have what the want in life.

Here's why.

If you could isolate a thought, spin it with positive energy and project it out to the universe, no doubt it would come back to you like a boomerang, fully manifested, instantly.

But the problem is that our thoughts don't live in a vacuum. Quite the opposite. At any one moment, our minds are filled almost to capacity with thoughts, feelings, memories, hopes, fantasies, fears, anxieties, projections and more. Our minds are incredibly rich with knowledge, data and experiences, lessons we've learned, conclusions we've drawn, attitudes, and reactions.

So if each of these thoughts has an energetic potential to magnetize its likeness, you can imagine how hard it is for any one of them to take shape in your reality. If thoughts are the medium for you to attract the experiences you want, then you can see how much competition you have for your dreams to come real. Like a solo violin trying to be heard above the roar of an entire orchestra, your well-intentioned thoughts about what you want in your life compete with the myriad of intentions and reactions in your mind, each resonating with its own fervor and feelings.

And so far, we've only mentioned the thoughts that you are conscious of! According to Sigmund Freud and Carl Jung, the subconscious mind and the unconscious mind contain vastly more content than what we perceive consciously. Freud used the terms "subconscious" and "unconscious" somewhat interchangeably, so we don't have to get too technical about their differences. He described the unconscious mind as our personal reservoir of traumatic memories, painful emotions, repressed urges and ideas ~ the stuff we don't usually process well on a conscious level. After years of research, Jung even broadened the definition further to include the 'collective unconscious': a layer of awareness that we share with the entire species.

So yeah, you have a whole universe of consciousness between your ears! Each thought — no matter its source, no matter when it was generated or why— each thought resonating with its own signature having the potential to attract its likeness into your experience. Now that's a lot of potential.

This is why *affirmations* — carefully-constructed positive phrases that express an intended outcome — don't live up to their promise.

Taking a cue from "Every day in every way," millions of people use affirmations to help them attract the experiences they want in their lives. To construct an affirmation, it is recommended that you keep it in the present tense. Use "I am" and "he is" statements instead of "I will" or "he will" ones that describe future events. The reason is that the mind lives only in the present, and an effective affirmation will reflect what is happening at any one moment in the present. Also, it is advised to avoid negatives of all kinds. Avoid the word "not" as in "not fat" and use "thin" or even "healthy" instead. The mind cannot grasp the *absence* of something, which is what "not" implies. You're wanting to manifest something that exists, not something that doesn't exist. Of course, always spin what might be a negative experience into its positive counterpart. Say "My mother-in-law has found the perfect place to live in town and is happy there" instead of "My mother-in-law isn't happy living with us and is moving out."

Here are a few examples of affirmations about topics common to many of us:

> *I am attracting my perfect love relationship into my life I am working at a new job I love and I'm earning $3000 per month I am losing weight and feeling good about myself*
>
> *My wife and I are saving enough money for a down payment on a new home My employees respect me and I am effective at work I am taking an hour for myself each day to unwind and relax I am healing my relationship with my mother and we are getting along I am eating healthy foods and my body feels energetic and strong*

You probably have tried it in one way or another. Maybe you've looked in the mirror and tried to convince yourself that you're beautiful or attractive or successful, and tried to ignore the knot in your gut, the hurt in your heart, or other tensions or discomforts you felt in your body that screamed "No way!" But if 'mind over matter' actually worked, you'd see the results in a matter of time. But mind over matter doesn't work, and for very good reason. In fact, recent research studies have shown that more often than not, when people use affirmations, the *opposite* happens to them. Why is that?

Here's what happens. When you assert something positive (even if you ARE beautiful or attractive or successful!) and if any part of you, hidden in your subconscious mind, disagrees with it, you are setting off a war within you over who's right. If you've got a number of parts of yourself that think the worst about yourself —most of us do — you're throwing down the gauntlet with all of those other parts of yourself. Even worse, by doing so, you fuel the very thoughts you want to conquer. Soon, you may notice that not only didn't things get better, but some of your worst fears actually came true in one way or another.

While the mirror exercise hasn't done much for anyone, it reveals a lot about how our minds work. After all, those screaming voices, contracted muscles and even waves of nausea are each parts of you expressing themselves and having something to say, too. They want to be heard, and won't go down without a fight if provoked! Ignoring them does not make them go away. And it shouldn't. Because all of those dissenting voices are parts of you that have been conceived and generated through your life experience (and possibly previous life experiences) and are there to help you avoid pain and suffering, to point out when danger is on the horizon. They are a part of your survival mechanism, and they are trying to be of service to you the only way they know how.

About 2400 years ago, a man named Siddhartha Gautama went on a spiritual path, determined not to stop until he was able to know for himself the true meaning of life. After years of meditation and sacrifice, he achieved a transcendent state of enlightenment, experiencing an unshakable, irrefutable, profound sense of oneness with the universe and an understanding of how life as we know it is created. After some prodding by his disciples, the man who would be known from then on as the *Buddha*, or enlightened one, agreed to teach others about what he had seen within himself. And what was the first point that he made?

Life is suffering.

Yup. Of all the profound truths he could feed his spiritually hungry followers, he started with that. It's what he told the throngs of seekers who had travelled for miles, most of them barefoot, living on a few grains of rice per day, meditating and seeking the wisdom of this great Master.

Here's how he described it: If you look closely at the workings of your own mind, you'll discover that it is always in a discord with what is. You are either wanting something you don't have, or *not* wanting what you do have. The grass always looks greener, the achievements you seek are ahead of you, the wife is making you unhappy today, the job doesn't quite fit, and so forth. In other words, we are interminably unhappy and 'suffering' because we want things to be other than the way that they are. We're constantly at odds with what is, not finding peace or contentment in the moment.

Much of what we have attracted in our lives is not done by deliberate intent, but comes about by default, as a result of what we have thought about and focused on in the past, whether we want it or not. Chronic thoughts about unwanted things invite, and attract, matching experiences.

So keeping a positive attitude is a very potent and important practice to lay the groundwork for working *with* the Law of Attraction. Since all of our thoughts generate our experiences, staying aware of when your thoughts go negative, and putting them back on a positive track will help to populate your future experiences with positive ones.

And by the way, don't allow yourself to beat yourself up if you have a tendency to go negative in life. That just adds another layer of self-judgment that does you no good. Do the best you can to stay positive and read on for more insights and practices to help you turn that around.

As a single method to attract specific experiences, people, achievements and things that we desire in our lives, thinking positively falls short. We'll explore what else is necessary to really propel your desires to become your new experience.

CHAPTER THREE

WHY TREASURE MAPS DON'T LEAD TO THE GOLD

It is by going into the abyss that you find your treasure

— Joseph Campbell

With our minds a jumbled cauldron of memories, feelings, conclusions and strategies, perceptions and reactions, patterns and habits, we have a task before us to single out a thought or two, project it onto the screen of the Universe, and dare to say — like Jean-Luc Picard aboard the Enterprise — "Make it so!"

Treasuring mapping is a tool that has gained popularity in this country to supposedly help people manifest what they want in life. Otherwise known as a vision board, the idea is to cut out photos and inspiring words from magazines or print out online images that you like that depict the things that you want to create in your life. Then arrange them in a pleasing way and paste them up on a poster board. When you're done, hang the board on the wall in plain view so that you can seed your subconscious mind with the images and get the law of attraction working for you.

Treasure maps frequently contain images of houses, smiling families, piles of cash, cars, exotic lands, and other desireables, along with uplifting words like "Empowerment" and "Live your dream!" And they can be helpful in a few ways. By keeping visual cues and reminders of what you want around you in your living or workspace helps you to *repeatedly* generate thoughts about your desired outcome. Repetition is one powerful practice that helps to activate The Law of Attraction and we'll discuss it further in Chapter 11.

The time you take and the steps you go through to create your treasure map can be valuable in getting the process started. By sorting through images, you are forced to define more precisely what it is you want to attract in the first place. Do you want a house with a yard or a porch? Or both? Do you want a new puppy that's small and cuddly or large and playful? Do you want to earn $1000 per month or $10,000? Just like when you go shopping in a store, the more you know about what you want, the easier it will be to find it.

As you take time to cull and categorize the images you want for your treasure map, you're bound to have a variety of feelings arise. You'll feel excited, perhaps, and inspired. More importantly, you might easily become aware that you have fears and reactions that you harbor about bringing the thing you want into your field of experience. That's useful! Notice what pushes your buttons. See if you can hear what some of the uninvited voices in your head say about your ability to obtain what you want. Or better yet, what are they saying about your worthiness or readiness for it? That's all good stuff!

Remember our lone violin, trying to be heard above an orchestral cacophony of other instruments, other voices, trying to bring something into being with the Law of Attraction? Joseph Campbell was right when he said: "It is by going into the abyss that you find your treasure." When we explore the abyss of our subconscious mind, we can free the treasure within. When we take the time to look into our limiting beliefs and negative thought patterns, our conditioned responses from years and years of learning and habit, we can quiet the din of dissenting voices and free up our ability to attract what we want. You can mute those out-of-tune voices that directly conflict with your desired outcome, shut down the ones that disempower your vision, quiet the ones that disempower you in general, and lay the groundwork to accelerate your effectiveness with the Law of Attraction.

But that's exactly why treasure maps rarely bring about an activation of the Law of Attraction, and why people rarely manifest what they have on their board.

Let's say you have a picture of a happy healthy, attractive couple, holding hands, staring at a picturesque sunset. And next to it, you have a picture of the BMW 335 that you've always wanted. Because these images are placed together, and when you see one, you see the others, your mind reads it as one single creation. It does not separate the picture of cash from the image of the couple from the image of the healthy athlete. For your mind, it becomes an all-or-nothing proposition. It's one creation, in a sense.

However, since you are a human being, chances are exceedingly high that you are going to have subconscious cultural conditioning about any (and likely all) of these objects of your desires. After all, you aren't currently enjoying these things in your life, which means that for one reason or another you have not been resonating with them. Their very absence is an indication that the parts of you that are pushing them away are winning over those parts that wanting to attract them. It could safely be said that your vision board is a map to the dissenting parts of you that do not want those things around! And it doesn't make for a much of a fertile field for attracting what you want.

Another shortcoming of vision boards and treasure maps is that they give some people a false sense that the board itself has magic powers to magnetize what they want. They might have the board hanging near their desk in their office or within view when they're lying in bed, but if they are not committing themselves to taking time to focus on each image, give attention and love to their vision, or feed it with energy, then the board isn't much more than a pretty picture on the wall. Even worse, it can lead people to forget that the power to create what they want is within *them* — all the time — not in something outside of themselves.

If you want to manifest a new home, a happy relationship, a healthy body, then make the most of the Law of Attraction as described herein. But start with one area of your life. Dig in and focus on one thing at a time and attend to it with love, patience, and humility along with the practices you'll learn in this book. The Universe is listening!

CHAPTER FOUR

FUELING THE ENGINE OF ATTRACTION

That's been one of my mantras — focus and simplicity.

—Steve Jobs

So if we essentially house a chaotic collection of an infinite number of thoughts and reactions in our consciousness — and since the life we live appears to be a fairly orderly one — how does the Universe select from all of those thoughts floating in our being and choose which ones to manifest in our lives?

I'm so glad you asked. For the answer is the first seed of empowerment, the beginning of living a life of choice and fulfillment.

The Law of Attraction responds to what we give most attention and energy to. It's what we spend the most time thinking about that invites and attracts matching experiences. Attention is focused consciousness, and with our consciousness we activate our thoughts, like strumming a guitar, and get them ringing with resonance. The more intensely we do so, and the more repeatedly we do so, the more loudly those strings will sound, and the greater power of resonance they will hold to attract an experience.

Bringing focus to a thought is the first step. Focusing on a thought or image can go a long way to make it stand out from the crowd. Spend a few minutes every day just focusing on what you want. It's no wonder that successful entrepreneurs like Steve Jobs sings the praises of focus as it keeps people aligned with their goals.

Then, to increase the resonance of a thought even further, bring emotion into the picture. Emotional energy juices a thought, resonating its potential, and gets it to 'sing' louder. Emotions, after all, can energize people to jump up and down with joy, paint a big smile on their face with happiness, or even hit a fist into a wall with anger. Emotions *are* essentially thoughts that have been excited and animated so much that we feel them in our bodies.

You can use any emotion to empower a thought; any emotion works as well as any other. Emotion is an equal opportunity energy source, and that can work for you or against you. On the one hand, it means that you have choices about what emotion you want to use. On the other hand, it means that fear is as effective as love and that anger is as effective as joy to magnetize experiences into your life. And you know what that means. When you obsess over your fears, and let them run rampant in your mind and body, you are essentially inviting whatever it is you fear to be made manifest, calling on the Law of Attraction to match your experience. Likewise, if you harbor anger, resentment or hatred towards others, for whatever reason that may seem justifiable to you, you are fueling the system to bring you more of exactly that which you are angry about. You are essentially asking for more of what you think you're rejecting.

Fear is a powerful emotion and probably fuels the vast majority of experiences we have on the planet. We have vast stores of fears in our subconscious mind, generated from our own life experiences, from the biases and expectations that we've absorbed from our culture and environment, from species memory, and potentially from an extensive set of recollections from past lives. If you look around at the stage settings of your life, and you find that much of it you don't want, you are seeing an expression of some of the fears that you harbor in your subconscious mind.

Anger is also a magnetic stimulant. Have you ever walked into a room and felt someone's anger even before you saw their face? It virtually emanates out of a person's skin. Anger can build and escalate and engage even innocent bystanders, igniting people it gets in proximity to. As an attracting medium, anger is potent. Like everything else in your experience, it is also reflecting something about you. If you find that you spend a lot of time around angry people, it is extremely likely that you harbor feelings of anger in yourself.

In later chapters, we'll discuss how you can use the cues from your outer experience like breadcrumbs on a trail, to help you find and bring to light some of the fears that are resonating from within your subconscious mind. By doing so, you can release them and release yourself from the grip they have on you.

Now that you know how emotions can light the spark of the Law of Attraction, use it wisely. First, select a thought of something you want to magnetize into your life. Start by focusing on it. Take some time with it and think about it without distraction. Set an intention to have it be center of your attention for a short while. Say No to interruptions or tempting diversions for that period of time.

Then add emotion. Think about what you want to attract in your life and allow yourself to get excited about it! Fill yourself with joy, relief, gratitude, and love. Take several minutes, repeatedly throughout the day and imagine what you want, feeling the enthusiasm and joy you'd feel from having what you are attracting in your life. Pump it up!

Add consistency and repetition. Focus and emotion can empower a thought, but not when done in isolation. You'll need to make it part of a consistent practice that you maintain over a period of time.

Don't forget love! Love is very likely the most powerful force in the Universe ~ so bring it into this practice! Fill your whole body and being with love as you think about what it is you want to attract into your life.

While there's a lot more to the Law of Attraction than these principles, they can be an immensely powerful place to start. With commitment, repetition and time, you'll be amazed at what you will attract into your life.

CHAPTER FIVE

The Choice that will Change Your Life

Whether you think you can or you think you can't, you're right.

—Henry Ford

All of the people, experiences, life events, and things that come to you in your life come as a response to the resonance of your thoughts, feelings and intentions. When you look around you now, you can get a picture of what you have invited into your life by way of vibrational resonance in the past. For whatever thoughts and ideas that you have given attention to, with focus, repetition, intensity or other factors, the Universe recognizes them as invitations and requests to manifest and attract into your life. Whether you think you want them or not.

Fortunately and unfortunately, what manifests doesn't manifest instantaneously. We've got a buffer of time between the point at which a powerful thought is projected and when it shows up in life. That time difference is part of what keeps us in the dark about how the Law of Attraction works. We don't see the cause directly followed by its effect, and when we do experience the effect, we don't know how to trace it to its cause. This time lag is an easy out: if every time you thought a negative thought, a brick fell out of the sky and hit you on the head, you'd clean up your thinking pretty fast.

Sometimes we start out with positive thoughts and beliefs, only to succumb to the beliefs of those around us, planting negative thoughts in our minds. A child may hold a healthy sense of her self-worth, for example, but if others around her repeatedly claim that she is less than that, she will eventually adopt that perspective and unconsciously resonate with it. After a while, she'll begin to attract evidence of it in her world, since it will be reflected in her outer reality soon enough, in effect now seeming to prove the lie to be true. Over time, she would not be able to distinguish the truth about her worthiness from what is false, for she will accumulate experiences in her life that act it out, and she'll want to believe what she is seeing.

Thinking negative thoughts and complaining about our experiences is very seductive but it focuses on what we don't want, fueling it. In the meantime, we think that our negative perspectives are the innocent result of us, like Monday morning quarterbacks, harmlessly judging our lives and experiences from an objective position and seeming to tell it like it is.

"The traffic is impossible today."

"I can't do anything right."

"My wife doesn't understand what I really need."

"I'm not good enough."

"This job is killing me."

These sentiments sure do seem to be true. But negative thinking and complaining focuses your mind and energy precisely on what you don't want. Many of us practice it religiously. If it gets to be a chronic activity, then the personality takes on a certain attitude and disposition that you identify with and that feels comfortable, but that continually emits negativity, attracting more negative circumstances to you. It also holds you in a position of pre-empting positive experiences and any of the actual solutions that you're looking for.

Try this out: Say out loud one of the complaints you frequently repeat to yourself. Then follow it with the words: "You're right." How does it feel? Depressing, right? But all you did was agree with yourself!

The Universe will always agree with you. It is always saying Yes to your vibrational wishes. It is always saying, "You're right."

So you get to decide what you want to be right about. After all, you're the one that keeps repeating these things over and over like a mantra. You are not a detached, objective witness of life, after all. You are a participant. What you say about the world, if it said with enough focus and energy, will come about in your field of experience. Now's the time to choose what you want to be true, what you want to experience and what you want to create for yourself in your life.

Negative thinking comes in other forms besides simply thinking negative thoughts. It can also do damage in the form of incessant problem-solving. Now, in the complex world we live in, there is of course a useful need and a place for solving everyday problems. But if your mind is filled all day with how to fix your health, your finances, your relationship, or something else, then you are actually getting in the way of the very solutions you seek. After all, just to get started looking for solutions to a problem, you invest quite a bit of energy into feeling helpless in the face of it, into investigating its moving parts, into looking at the variables. You are committing yourself to the perception that it is a problem in the first place. While the pain and suffering of the situation may be very real for all those involved, the negative attention does not help you create the improved outcome you want to see in your life.

So try a different approach. Set aside 15 minutes a day and visualize the painful situation resolved and the problem healed. As you imagine it, fill yourself with a positive feeling like joy and gratitude. After all, how great would you feel if you were living that reality? Bask in those good feelings as you envision your desired outcome: your body healed, your rent paid, a relationship harmonized, or whatever you desire. Avoid visualizing with the intention of correcting what is wrong or deficient, because if you do, your thoughts will be diluted with the negative side of the equation. Instead of fueling the problem, trying to figure out how to fix it, imagine the best possible outcome you want for yourself.

Then, the next time you find yourself complaining about the situation, flip into visualizing the healed experience you want to create. Bathe in feelings of exuberance, joy, and gratitude as you imagine yourself in the new reality. Keep activating your 'choice' muscle, releasing the negative reactions and stepping into the positive experience of your visualization. It may seem challenging at first: you've likely got a very well-ingrained, habitual thinking pattern. But when you think about it, you realize that no one is making you feel what you're feeling. Quite the opposite: you have an infinite array of choices of how you can respond to the situation you're in. Regardless of how intense the feeling feels or how true the thoughts sound, you have the power to choose.

Negative thinking can also do its damage through other, less obvious ways we act, such as manipulation and control. When you try to make your circumstances better by trying to control or manipulate other people, you are actually banking on the negativity of the situation. Of course, there are certainly experiences in life that are frustrating and disempowering, and it is easy to come to the conclusion that the only way to get what you want or need is to manipulate others. But when you feel compelled to control or manipulate others, you are being driven by underlying, unconscious beliefs that claim that you are less than you are. They'll tell you that you are not powerful enough, not important enough, or not good enough to simply ask for and get what you want. Or that you don't have what it takes to receive the kindness, attention or benefit that the person you're trying to control seems to withhold from you. These underlying thoughts and beliefs lie in your subconscious mind, driving your experience, seeding your unhappiness, and motivating your controlling behavior.

But like the Chinese finger puzzle, the more you push, pull or manipulate, the more you are trapped, and the further away you get from achieving what you want. In other words, when you try to get what you want through coercive behavior, you are empowering the very seed thoughts that put you in your experience in the first place, setting yourself up to live through more of it in your future. Your attention to them brings more like them into your experience. You simply cannot get to where you want to be by controlling or eliminating the unwanted.

So what choice do you have?

Your choice — in every moment — is to be a co-creator of your life, and not just a victim of your experiences, which are after all the manifestation of your very own thoughts, feelings and beliefs. You may not be able to change the past, but you can change your future; what you think about and focus on now invites and attracts your future experiences.

Right now — each now moment — is the most powerful moment you have, and in each moment you can make the most powerful choice a human being can make in life: to be a co-creator of your life, rather than just a victim of your circumstances. You empower yourself by taking responsibility for your thoughts, feelings, energy and focus of attention. And you set the intention in each moment to raise your awareness, to be more conscious of what you think and feel, and to choose a positive vibe over a negative one.

You have the choice to allow yourself to feel your feelings this time, instead of stuffing them, ignoring them or even trying to make them go away with food, alcohol, prescriptions, drugs, risky behavior, television, or any other unconscious behavior. Give the feeling the attention it is asking for and bring the light of your awareness to it. Within every feeling is a seed thought; a feeling has a source and it is a thought. For example, you don't just feel sadness in isolation. You feel sad *that* something has occurred. You feel sad usually because you perceive loss in your life and you feel not whole because of that loss. Similarly, you don't feel anger in isolation. You feel anger *because* something happened. Anger is often a 'cover' feeling that obscures more intense feelings of helplessness or hurt.

Give yourself the compassion you need by spending a few moments being present to these kinds of feelings. You don't have to bask in the feelings or belabor them. You don't have to dramatize them or create a story around them. Those things don't help. You want to introduce yourself to the feeling and let it introduce itself to you. Oftentimes, with healthy attention, the feeling will subside and you can get back to your positive attitude.

It's completely counterintuitive, of course: facing the feelings that are at best uncomfortable, and at worst, excruciating. But like the proverbial monster in the closet, there really isn't anything solid behind the scary façade that your darker emotions project. Bringing the light of your awareness to these feelings weakens their power, and loosens you from their grip. Asking yourself any of the following questions can help:

> *Where is the feeling located in my body? If I rated it 1-10 in intensity, what would it be right now? If it had a color, what would that be? What is the feeling trying to say to me? What experiences does it remind me of?*

For highly intense and chronic feelings, you may want to use one or more of the numerous release techniques that are designed to help you extract all the unconscious tendrils of your heavier emotions from your subconscious mind and heal them. Methods like the Emotional Freedom Technique, EMDR, Thought Field Therapy, the HART technique, somatic practices, forgiveness practices and others can be tremendously helpful. Or you may choose to see a professional therapist to help you dig deep and get out from under the weight of some of your emotional burdens. Whatever method you choose, it will help you reconnect with the peace and wellbeing within you. Let it be part of your greater commitment to bring awareness to all that you are.

So while you keep a positive attitude, you are catching your negative thinking as it happens, choosing to focus and bring energy to the positive things in your life and imagining the joyful, healed, positive experiences that you want to create. You are embracing what is in the present moment, as it happens to show up.

And you are taking responsibility for your entire range of thoughts and feelings. You aren't just trying to sow positive seeds in an already-dense garden of negativity. You're pulling up the weeds as you go, looking at what's there, deciding what stays and what goes, so you can enjoy a field of positive vibes that flourish throughout your life. You're doing great!

CHAPTER SIX

What You Really Want To Attract

At the center of your being you have the answer; you know
who you are and you know what you want.

—Lao Tzu

The big thing is that you know what you want.

—Earl Nightingale

You're probably thinking that you already know what
you want to attract and manifest in your life, right? You
wouldn't be reading this book if you didn't have some thoughts in
your head about wanting a new relationship or a new car, a new
job or better health. So why this chapter? The Law of Attraction
works best if you know what you want. Like ordering a meal at
a restaurant, you don't want to wait until the food finally arrives,

only to say "Oh, that's not what I wanted!" This chapter will help you get a clearer sense of what you *really* want, and revs up your powers of attraction.

Besides, the Universe is wiser than all of us put together. So, if you go about 'asking' for something, trying to get the Law of Attraction working for you, but other parts of you, perhaps higher and wiser parts of you, don't really think it's the best thing for you, well, it just won't show up in your life. Your higher self and other parts that aren't in agreement with you will trump your efforts. But if you take time to see what your heart really desires, the stars are much more likely to align with your wishes.

The irony is, it's really super easy to know what you *don't* want. Just look at your long list of life complaints. You know exactly what you don't want. Yet, of course, if you harp on those negative perspectives, you feed the vicious cycle of reacting to the very experience that you yourself have set in motion with your thoughts and vibrations. So you get more of the same. And then you complain some more. And then you get more of the same....

But the list of what you don't want can actually be a good place to start to figure out what you *do* want. Check it out for yourself. Make a list of the top ten things in your life that you don't want. Then, for each one, flip it around and write down *what would be present* if you had it the way you wanted it.

For example:

I don't want my boyfriend to look at other women
becomes
I want to be in a happily monogamous relationship
I don't want my job to exhaust me so much
becomes
I want to have fun and be energized by my job
I don't want to have to worry about money
becomes
I want to be financially comfortable and secure

This is an extremely valuable step because your mind cannot conceive of the *absence* of something. (Try it. Try *not* thinking about a cut on your finger. For as long as you attempt it, another part of your mind is checking in and asking: "Am I thinking about the cut on my finger?" Gotcha.) So as long as you are asking the Universe to take something away from your experience, you are not going to create a resonance of what you do want. You'll just be reminding the Universe, and bringing attention to, what you don't want. This exercise gets you to formulate and clarify what you do want to create in your life so that you can focus on and attract it.

We are *not* suggesting that you use these statements as affirmations, by the way. These are just starter ideas to help you begin to get a sense of what you really want. Even more importantly, they help paint the picture of what you want to *experience* in your life. We're going to take that and run with it later to help you energize and bring to life the thoughts that describe what you most want.

Here's the secret: almost everything you want, you want because you think it will give you a certain *feeling*. Feelings like esteem, confidence, sense of worth and value, feelings of importance and significance, feelings of approval or being attractive. Or feelings of peace, contentment, and joy. What we really want, underneath it all, is to feel good in all of its variations.

Thankfully, the Law of Attraction feeds on full-body, juiced up feelings to put your request into play. So as you define what you want, you define what feeling you want to go for to activate the Law of Attraction.

Check it out: Let's say you think you really, really want a 2002 red Corvette Z06. You've done your research. You've compared features and you've taken one for a test-ride. You *know* that you would be so happy with that car! But would you be? Let's find out.

Ask yourself: *What is it that I want to feel by having this car?* For sure, it would be a lot of fun to drive! But what else would you want the car to help you feel? Successful? Important? Arrived? Impressive? Sexy? Attractive? Powerful? Did you just say "Yes" to all of those? Um hum, sure you did! But, logically speaking, do you really think that you can extract feelings of success, importance, sexiness, power and all the rest from a piece of machinery, as beautiful as might be? You might feel those things temporarily, but surely if some tragedy happened in your life, you wouldn't feel them for long.

Of course, you can't get those feelings just by associating with the vehicle. But it is tremendously valuable to know that these are feelings that you lack and that you are seeking to fill. And to be happier in life, you'll want to find meaningful ways to validate those feelings within you, from within. You might even discover that you want to focus on experiencing more of those feelings with the help of the Law of Attraction, even more than the car. Either way, they are the emotions you'll want to resonate and pulsate with when it's time to do your Law of Attraction work.

Next question: *If I were to already feel successful, important, arrived, sexy, etc., would I still want the car?* One thing is very likely: if you already felt those things, you probably won't feel like you *need* the car as much as you do otherwise.

If you are having financial troubles and you're stressed about money, it will be very helpful for you to clarify for yourself what you really want so that you can finally lift the burdened feelings you carry. So ask yourself: *What is it that you think you want, financially speaking?* A raise? A new job? A windfall? That's all well and good, but let's see if it passes the endurance test: If a miracle were to occur tomorrow and you got what you want, it would surely feel great. But if a catastrophe were to occur the following day, and the raise or the job fell through, you'd end up in the same emotional boat as you're in today. It is much more effective to aim for the underlying *feeling tone* of what you want in your life. As we demonstrated in the previous exercise, it likely reflects the deeper truth of what you really want. What feeling tone do you want to manifest in your life? Some people refer to it as "financial stability and security" or "financial comfort, support and ease." Use that or another phrase that feels right for you.

A lot of people think that what they really want is money. But you won't have to dig very deep to discover that most people have parts of themselves that *don't* want money. Most of us unconsciously hold numerous negative beliefs about money, all of which will fight your attempts to attract "money" into your life. Think of what you may have picked up subconsciously from movies, books and the internet, or from your parents, siblings or grandparents who most likely were just trying to give you some wisdom in life. Read through the list below and see if you have absorbed any of the following limiting (untrue) beliefs. As you read each one, pay attention to your body signals. If you experience a tightening of your gut, tension in our jaw, your heart feeling more heavy, or any similar physical responses, take note. A part of you agrees with what you're reading.

Money doesn't grow on trees
Rich people are bad, selfish or coldhearted

It's wrong to be selfish
If I have a lot, other people have less
Other people will suffer if I get what I want
It's not spiritual or Godly to be wealthy
It is easier for a camel to go through the eye of a needle than
for a rich man to enter the kingdom of God
You have to work hard to earn your keep
Money is a big responsibility and I can't handle it

It will be extremely helpful for you to clear and heal as many of these beliefs that you took on as a part of your social conditioning. The techniques mentioned in Chapter 5 and others like them can help you do this.

Here's another way to discover what you really want for yourself in your life. Do you ever feel any pangs of jealousy or envy when you hear about the successes of other people? Do you ever feel badly about yourself when you find out about someone else's victories or joys in life? These are clues to what you are wanting for yourself. In either case, ask yourself what it is that the other person seems to be feeling that you want to feel? And what would you be doing if you could imagine yourself feeling that? Now *that's* something your heart is really wanting.

The last gate of exploration into what you really want is to ask yourself what your heart most desires. No matter how well you work with the Law of Attraction or how much energy and effort you put into it, if your heart is not aligned with what you ask for, you won't attract it. So do some soul searching and meditate on what your heart really wants for you. In your heart of hearts, maybe you're feeling that a new car is not for your highest good at this point in time after all. Maybe there's an important lesson to learn at your workplace and a deeper part of you feels that it's best to stick it out a little longer. Or maybe you have an inner knowing that it would serve you best to heal some of your codependencies before you hook up with the next new relationship.

Again, by getting a sense of what *feeling tone* you want to expand and experience more in your life, you can't go wrong. In the case of the new car, maybe what you're really wanting are feelings of *safety, ease, grace and being taken care of,* when you're traveling here and there to do the things that you do to take care of yourself. You can focus on those as the feeling tone of what you want in your life. If your workplace is uncomfortable, perhaps the feeling tone you want to have for yourself is *belonging, respect and harmony* and you can focus on attracting those. If you have codependencies, you might be well served to deepen your feelings of *honoring and valuing yourself* and feeling *good enough.*

Finding out what you really want deep down will help you attract what you really want. Doing so will help to bring you those experiences that express the feeling tones that matter the most to you.

CHAPTER SEVEN

ELIMINATING SELF-SABOTAGE

Your only problem is that you're too busy holding on to your unworthiness.

—Ram Dass

W e've already discussed in some measure the role that negative, limiting thoughts can play in defeating our attempts to attract what we want into our lives. While on one level, we can become aware of the thoughts that lie more on the surface of our consciousness, and shift them from a negative spin to a positive one. But on a a deeper level, we have untold numbers of thoughts in our subconscious and unconscious minds, many of which keep us stuck in old patterns in our day-to-day experiences. Entrenched in our lower consciousness, they hold tremendous sway in our life experience as they create opposite, resonance-canceling vibrations that disrupt the good vibes of our fledgling positive intentions. But we can turn the tables and take back our power from these troublemakers. Instead of relegating them to the netherworlds of our subconscious mind, we can take steps to bring them to light, heal some of the most cumbersome ones, and clear the air for the thoughts we want to empower and spin into our new reality.

There are three belief/feeling states that we in the Western world are especially vulnerable to and that play havoc with our attempts to live a joyful, creative, fulfilled life. These are unworthiness, shame and lack.

While these feelings and the beliefs that underpin them run rampant in our culture, they are not innate to all human psychology. They are not natural, not required, and not necessary. They are more simply a set of psychological patterns that we have absorbed from our human environment, adopting them into our psyches. But they don't serve our happiness, our worthiness or our highest good. And thankfully, they can be healed.

The belief in one's own unworthiness is ubiquitous in our society. It usually comes from feelings of anger, blame or fear turned inward. It's a way that we attack ourselves and repeatedly punish ourselves with all the force we can rally. You may have been abused or neglected as a child and came away with the unconscious conclusion that you were treated that way instead of being loved because you weren't worthy of it. That's one way that the psyche survives traumas: by drawing conclusions — right or wrong — that help make a situation make sense. Or you may have been given the message from family members, teachers or religious leaders, either directly and verbally or indirectly and nonverbally, that you weren't worthy of love or acceptance or belonging. And you buried that belief in your mind as a reference point for survival in the future. Or you may have been ashamed about things you've done or situations you've experienced, and you funneled those feelings into a sense of unworthiness.

The important thing to remember about unworthiness is that it is not a state of mind or a state of being. It is something that you tell yourself or that you believe. It is not a truth; it is a perspective. And like any perspective, it can be replaced with a higher, more truthful one.

What's more, underneath your belief in your own unworthiness, if you have it (and most of us do) is a great and deep sorrow. For when you let yourself believe in your own unworthiness, you unknowingly, innocently, unwittingly betrayed the truth of your self: that you are unlimited, infinite, powerful and glorious. And that you are, and you have, all that you need. By embracing the illusion of your own unworthiness, you turned away from something very, very important: *you*. The shame of this existential turning pervades the consciousness of so many of us. But it can be healed.

In her groundbreaking book, Daring Greatly, Brenée Brown defines shame as "the intensely painful feeling or experience of believing that we are flawed and therefore unworthy of love and belonging." Feelings of shame and thoughts about one's unworthiness often go hand in hand; where one is seen, the other is likely to be nearby. Those who are convinced of their own terribly flawed nature, inflict shame upon themselves as a matter of course, repeatedly, and punishingly. And that won't leave much room for attracting loving, satisfying, joyful or successful experiences in life.

The belief in lack is another pervasive and corrosive perspective that underlies the consciousness of most of us. You can see it in action in feelings of competition and jealousy, and in fears about limited money, ability, time or potential. But there are very few real limits in life; you have an unlimited array of choices in each moment.

It will serve you greatly to heal these powerful unconscious feelings and beliefs — unworthiness, shame, and lack — for they will undermine your attempts to attract what you want in life and they will undermine your very joy and happiness. Find ways to forgive yourself and have compassion for yourself as a human being who is doing your best in a world that doesn't give you a user manual to guide you around all the sand traps it can put in your path. Forgive yourself for being human and give yourself the compassion you are truly worthy of.

Use meditation and awareness tools to undermine the hold that beliefs in unworthiness, shame and lack have on you. Engage in healing practices or work with professional therapists and practitioners to dig deep and get to the bottom of the subconscious beliefs that drive most of what you do and most of what you feel. Discover the freedom of releasing them from your fundamental emotional and mental coding.

When you clear these underlying premises in your psyche, your world will shift dramatically. You will begin to give yourself far more permission to live a life of success, joy, love and fulfillment. You'll find things you want coming your way more easily as the dampening vibes of unworthiness no longer play out. You'll find a lot more love reflected in your world as you resonate with more self-love, freed from the grip of unconscious negative beliefs and perspectives. And your focused work with the Law of Attraction will be supercharged!

Let's see if we can uproot some feelings of lack right here. Ask yourself the following question:

Exactly how much happiness am I willing to accept from the Universe?

Be honest. The question is to be asked of *all* of you, all parts of you, so let it sink in first. What's your answer? And how freely, unequivocally, immediately, and fully did you answer the question with: "As much as it will give me!" Or did you answer the question with hesitation or doubt, weakness or uncertainty? If you are not 100% all in on this one, as your true answer to the question, then there are parts of you that are working against your very abundance. Let's take a closer look.

Let's dig deeper. How would you answer any of these questions related to living a life of abundance and prosperity?

Are you worthy of it?

Are you deserving of it?

Are you ready for it?

Are you capable of handling it?

Would it be wrong or selfish for you to accept it lavishly?

Do you think others will have less if you have more?

Would you feel guilty if you were rich?

If you answered No to any of the first four questions or Yes to any of the last three questions, then you are holding untrue, negative beliefs in your consciousness that will pretty effectively limit your ability to attract abundance and prosperity. Try having a heart-to-heart with yourself and talk out these feelings and beliefs. Be the devil's advocate and the angel's advocate too. Let the parts of you that feel undeserving, not ready, and so forth have their say and express themselves. (Do this one part at a time. Don't try to do several at once, if possible.) Then come back as your own nurturing parent, and reassure that part of you that he or she *is* deserving, or *is* ready. See if you can let the intensity and feeling dissipate until the false belief no longer feels true in any way.

To counteract any tendency you have to see the glass as half-empty, to see yourself lacking, choose to take on an attitude of abundance. See the richness of life all around you. And be grateful for it. See the infinite ways in which you are being taken care of, pampered, loved, heard, supported and embraced in your life. And be grateful for them. Get your heart to smile more. Appreciate the details in everything and everyone, including yourself.

If you experience a lot of jealousy and enviousness of other people and their possessions — or their successes, or their happiness — here's how to unravel it. Write a list of all of the people that you have any sort of jealousy towards, anyone who brings up thoughts in you that you are less than they are. Ready? Title the list: "I Am Grateful For Your Success!" Then look at each name on your list and choose to feel gratitude for their possessions, their successes and their happiness. If they have brought wonderful experiences into their lives, that means that you can too. The Law of Attraction is an equal-opportunity principle, remember? So fill yourself with gratitude and tell the Universe — and mean it! — that you are grateful for the success that the people on your list allowed themselves to actualize in their lives. It is a blessing that it is possible at all. Do this practice every day, keeping your list updated with new names as you discover your mind targeting them with jealousy or envy. Notice how your heart is lifted when you do this, and your capacity for happiness expands.

The point is that your joyful feelings are the measure of your capacity to receive what you want. Do we need to repeat that? Your joyful feelings are the measure of your capacity to receive what you want. So fill yourself with joy. Find reasons to be grateful and joyful; find reasons to feel appreciative and fortunate. The Universe is listening. And, as we know, the Universe is reflecting back to you the thoughts and feelings that you hold and express. So amp it up a notch, generate more pleasant feelings, and watch how your world starts to feel more prosperous, more magical and more abundant.

CHAPTER EIGHT

TAKING IT TO THE NEXT LEVEL

Imagination is the beginning of creation. You imagine what you desire, you will what you imagine and at last you create what you will.

—George Bernard Shaw

Visualize this thing that you want, see it, feel it, believe it, make it your mental blueprint and begin to build.

—Robert Collier

We've already said that energizing a thought can empower it to manifest. Once you have faced some of your fears, released many of the limiting and sabotaging thoughts in your consciousness, and clarified what you really want, then the thought is fortified and is better able to take root and express itself lavishly in your life experience.

Now you're ready to take it to the next level. Now it really gets fun!

Life is energy and you are an energy generator. You are an astounding being with the capacity to come up with a thought, focus on it, create a swirl of energy with it, intensify it, and bring it to life! The Tuning Fork exercise, described below, guides you to do this. When you do the exercise, you're going to visualize the thought and image of what you want. Then you'll build up an energy bath around it, charge yourself up like a battery, vibrate with it and resonate with it until your being is singing like a tuning fork.

Before you get started with the exercise, take the following steps so that you've got all cylinders pumping and working in your favor:

• Create an experience

Expand the idea of what you want to attract into your life into a three-dimensional virtual-reality *experience*. For example, if you want a new car that costs $25,000, what is it that you want to experience with that car? Maybe you want to imagine it all shiny and beautiful in your garage or in your driveway, as you stand there admiring it, proud of your accomplishment? Or maybe what really turns you on is the idea of driving along the coastline with your girlfriend in the passenger seat? (If you don't have a girlfriend or spouse right now, then it's best to leave one out of this picture for now. Otherwise, you're trying to magnetize two realities and that can slow everything down at this stage.)

• Animate it

Get a sense of what you might do in the experience that would be congruent with it. For example, if you want to attract a love relationship, and it were to materialize *now*, you might be sitting and talking with each other, dancing at a local music venue, or enjoying a meal at a restaurant. You're going to want to throw a few different scenes into the pot of your visualization to animate it and activate it.

• Get clear on the feelings associated with the experience

What are the feelings you'll likely feel once you have the red corvette? Exuberance, excitement, pleasure, joy? Exactly. If you're wanting to have more money in your bank account, then the feelings associated with it might be financial stability, a sense of security, feeling taken care of. If you want to manifest better physical health, then the associated feelings might be aliveness, pleasure, expansion, and self-sufficiency. Remember these feelings. You'll use them in the exercise.

• Don't confuse the means with the ends

Sometimes people confuse the end result of what they want with the means, tools, or steps it might take to achieve it. For the purposes of the visualization exercise below, you'll want to project out to the Universe the final result of what you want in all its glory, and let the Universe figure out the best way for that to come about. So if you're desiring that red corvette, then it's the car itself that you want to experience in your life, not the $25,000 that it would likely cost to purchase it. Focus on the car, not the money. If you want good health and wellness in your body, then visualize that, not the medicines, exercise or other regimens that might get you there. You're going to project the "what" of what you want and let the Universe figure out the "how." It works in mysterious ways, after all.

• Have fun with it

Do other things to enhance feelings of expectation and excitement about bringing the experience you want into your life. You can journal about all the things you want to do with your new-found health or your new place to live. You can create a mini treasure map of images that get you enthused and then review them with relish regularly. You can talk to supportive friends and share your vision and ideas, and ask them to get excited with you.

• Be grateful in advance

Open your heart with gratitude for the experience that you are about to have. Let the gratitude swirl in your heart and then swell out to others around you. Thank everyone and everything that is making it possible for what you want to be in your life. Including yourself. Gratitude is love and love is the most powerful force in the Universe!

The Tuning Fork Exercise

Warning! This is a powerful practice! If you have not done the work described in earlier chapters to heal and release sabotaging thoughts, beliefs and withheld emotions, this step might bring stuff up for you! Make sure you do some soul-searching so that as much of you as possible is aligned with creating what you want. This works!

Imagine yourself in the experience you want to create and really immerse yourself in it. Let yourself see your surroundings, hear the sounds of the people, animals or other things that around you in the scene. See yourself moving around, interacting with others, doing what you would do in the experience you want to bring to yourself. What you're doing is visualizing an entire scene for what you want, and creating a virtual-reality experience right in your own body. Let yourself step into the arena of what you are creating and let it build an aura of its own.

Page through a few scenes of the experience, imagining yourself engaged in a few activities that include or revolve around the new reality that you're attracting into your life. As you do so, feel the feelings you've identified earlier. Fill your body and being with excitement, joy and gratitude. Especially gratitude.

Let the intensity increase. Let the feelings expand, swirl, and rise. Enjoy the pleasure of the feelings for several minutes. Notice how real it feels. End with more gratitude.

*   *   *

Important: As you do this exercise, if you notice parts of you protesting — contraction in your gut, heaviness in your heart, headaches, confusion, or other uncomfortable feelings — then stop what you're doing and re-group. These are cues from your subconscious mind that one or more parts of you are not in alignment with what you are focusing on to create. Honor these parts of yourself and take the time to investigate before resuming the exercise. Do NOT try and push through it. Your subconscious mind is quite powerful and will have its way one way or the other. So take some time to do any of the release techniques described or mentioned earlier in this book. If the feelings persist, you may want to seek help from a health professional.

*   *   *

Congratulations! You are now beginning to master the Law of Attraction! You are surely seeing results in your life and attracting more of what you desire. Great! There's just one more step to really bring it home.

CHAPTER NINE

THE SECRET OF SURRENDER

The creative process is a process of surrender, not control.

—Julia Cameron

There's an old parable about a man who lived in a small town that one day was besieged with emergency warnings about a terrible storm coming its way. The local officials ordered everyone to evacuate immediately. But the man decided to stay put, saying to himself, "I will trust God, for I know that God will send a divine miracle to save me."

On their way out of town, some neighbors stopped by and offered him a ride in their car, but the man turned it down, saying, "No thanks. God will save me."

As the man stood on his porch watching the waters turn into rivers, a friend paddled by in his canoe and pleaded with the man to join him and save himself. But the man again said, "No thanks! God will save me!"

The floodwaters surged and the man was forced to retreat to the second floor of his house. A police motorboat puttered by his window. They shouted to him that they could rescue him from the rising waters, but the man refused their help, saying, "I have faith that God will help me!"

The waters swelled higher and the man had to climb onto his roof. A helicopter spotted him and dropped a rope ladder for him to climb to safety. Once again, the man refused any help.

So the man drowned. And when he got to heaven, he asked God, "I put my faith in you. Why didn't you save me?" And, of course, God said, "Gosh, I sent you a warning, a car, a canoe, a motorboat and a helicopter. What exactly were you waiting for?"

* * *

This delightful story depicts the truth of so many of us. Aren't most of us oblivious to the gifts that the Universe is sending us all of the time? Aren't we sometimes unaware of the uncountable ways that we are taken care of? Remember: the Universe is listening — and responding —to everything you are asking for, consciously, subconsciously, and unconsciously at every moment. Are you noticing?

There's another, more subtle message to this fine tale, as well. That is: *You are not alone.* You are partnered with the Universe to co-create your experience and manifest your dreams. Any time you find yourself efforting too hard, problem-solving, and worrying, you are forgetting that it is not for you to conceive and generate your experiences all by yourself. You are forgetting that you have an immensely powerful, invisible partner in this journey of your life with you. While you are here on this planet to create and experience your unique human identity, you are in a dance with the infinite forces of the Universe to do just that. *You are not alone.*

Yet most of us act as if we are in this thing called life, alone, most of the time. Maybe we consult our spouse or parent or respected friend and share the burdens of decision-making and taking care of our needs. Even so, we spend most of our waking hours taking actions and making decisions unilaterally. Some confuse 'being responsible' with taking care of things themselves, and they don't think to consult their invisible partner to help them when they need it. But they could.

You can call it your ego: that sense of having a unique, independent, separate identity that lives somewhere between your ears and that makes the judgments, draws the conclusions, designs the strategies and makes the decisions in your life. Up until this point, just about everything that you've wanted to attract into your life has been driven by the desires of your ego, motivated by the fears of your ego, and limited to the finite conceptual perspectives of the mind of your ego. It's not a bad thing. It's simply part of being human, after all. It's just that it has limited scope to really manifest a glorious life for you.

But there's another way to work with the Law of Attraction besides taking the role of single petitioner, trying to wrestle a few more bits of gold to enjoy in life from the Universe's supposed goldmine of potential. Or only trying to satisfy the pleasures and appease the fears of your ego. Instead of projecting images out to the Universe like letters to Santa Claus, hoping the things you want will show up, just as you imagined, all ribboned and ready to unwrap, you can use the power of the Universe to bring you what you most want in an even more powerful way. You can live an evolved partnership with the Universe, letting the Universe decide what is best, how is best and when is best. That's when surrender comes into play and that's when the magic really happens.

The idea of surrender freaks some people out because they think it requires that they give up control. But you will always have complete control over how much control you want to give up. In fact, you're always in control; you just get to choose what it is you want to surrender! It's just that when you choose to hand things over, you are no longer the Boss of the issue or the

Supervisor of the creation. It's not your personal achievement any longer; you're simply the junior partner along for the ride.

And what freedom that is!

As far as the Law of Attraction is concerned, when you surrender to the spiritual forces of the Universe, you surrender your insistence that you know what is best. You're no longer the end-all be-all of what you're creating. Instead, you ask the Universe to engage its Wisdom and manifest what is best for the Highest good, whatever that may be. You admit you don't know everything and that Something Else knows more. You also surrender the demand that things have to happen on your timetable. Instead, you let things unfold in Divine time. Finally, you let go of your silly insistence that A has to happen before B and B before C, and instead you allow things to evolve in their highest order, in their highest way. You bow to the clear truth: the Universe knows best!

The secret of surrender is that when you turn your desires and wishes over to Higher Forces, you are no longer simply focused on your own personal happiness, seeking your own personal sunrise. You engage your spiritual heart and open yourself to the highest and best for all. You sign up with the Universe to do what is best for the Highest Good and Greatest Good for *all*, not just yourself. And this step will supercharge your ability to manifest — but only when you really mean it!

Here's another thing that will happen when you surrender. When you let go of trying to get what you want as your personal achievement, you won't coddle it and worry about it and stress over it as much. You won't obsess over it and micro-manage it. After all, guess what kind of vibes those things resonate with! Right! They are drenched with the negative vibes that interfere with and nullify your attempts to manifest what you desire in your life.

HERE'S THE SECRET FORMULA:

- *In times of struggle, ask the Universe for guidance about what to do instead of going it alone. Let the answers come to you in any form, at any time. Someone you know may give you the perfect advice, maybe you get a message through something you see online, maybe it just pops into your head. There are unlimited ways guidance can come to you. Stay open.*

- *Ask that all you do is of service to the Highest Good*

- *Ask that what you want comes in a way that is for the Highest Good for you and everyone concerned*

- *Ask that things come as you ask, or better, according to what is its highest expression*

- *Ask for the welfare, health, fulfillment and joy for your family and friends*

- *Ask for the health, safety and welfare of all the people in the country, the hemisphere or the planet*

- *Ask that you be an open vessel of love on the planet*

Love. The most powerful force on the planet. If you were to resonate with love all of the time, and resonate all that you desire with love, then the Law of Attraction would be child's play in your hands. The funny thing about love is that we are culturally conditioned to think that to 'love' means to hold on to something. You fall in love with someone and you want to marry them and be with them for the rest of your life. You see something at the store that you love and you want to take it home and own it. But love can also be profoundly expressed through letting go: letting your child go off to college, letting your friend have different likes than you, giving something that you cherish as a gift to someone you love. As far as the Law of Attraction is concerned, you embrace your desires with love, and then lovingly let go of them. You hand it over to the Universe to be returned to you in the perfect reflection of love.

Now go for it!

CHAPTER TEN

LIVING THE LAW OF ATTRACTION

Most of us are just about as happy as we make up our minds to be.

—William Adams

We are culturally conditioned to seek happiness from things outside of ourselves: in the friends we have, the car we drive, the fashionable clothes we wear, the successes we achieve, the house we inhabit, and/or the money we have in the bank. In so doing, the majority of us keep waiting through each moment of our lives for our outer circumstances to make us happy: for better health, a more attractive body, a loving relationship, a better job, and so forth. But in so doing we confuse the cause and effect of how things really work. It is happiness that generates our good experiences, not the other way around. The Law of Attraction wouldn't work if it were any other way.

In fact, you are the architect of your reality. The blueprints are in your hands and the design is being developed with each breath you take and each thought you think. Everything you experience comes from within your own being and the Law of Attraction is the medium that allows that to happen.

The Law of Attraction begins and ends with choosing the thoughts, feelings, attitudes and resonance that you embody every moment and every day. It's a deeper practice than thinking positive thoughts; it's a choice to keep re-choosing a positive attitude, a positive perspective, and positive feelings. Over and over and over and over again. One of the fastest ways to set the stage for the Law of Attraction is to focus on any subject — no matter what it is — that consistently feels good to you. This creates a foundation of positive feelings that will support you attracting whatever it is you want.

Use the tools described in this book to hone your skills and to forge your consciousness into a positive vessel for the Law of Attraction. Do your homework and clear your subconscious and unconscious sabotage patterns that get in the way of you having what you want in your life. Use whatever techniques support you to resonate and sing with positive vibes. Visualize what you want to attract in 3-D and bring as much passion and juice to it as you can. Then let it go, and give the whole intention up to the Universe to decide to bring it to you in the best and highest way.

Living the Law of Attraction isn't just about being positive; it's about being *present*. That means getting out of your head and into the lush expanse and abundance of everything around you: your very own co-creation. Aligning with the Law of Attraction is putting yourself on a path of consciousness and of deepening spirituality. You can't ignore the Universe and its presence in your life, your heart and your mind, when you begin to work closely with the Law of Attraction, for It is the Master Player on the other side of the ping pong table, playing along with you, reflecting back to you, building your life with you. More than that, the Universe (otherwise known as Spirit, your Higher Self, God, Allah, Yahweh, Great Spirit, or whatever you choose to call It) can become your guide to finding the highest and deepest joy and bliss that a human can come to know.

To get the most out of the Law of Attraction, choose to be at peace with what is, instead of being at war with it. Whenever possible, be more present to your experience, instead of reacting to it. Transform the challenges of your current experience by letting go of your habituated negative perspectives about what is making you suffer — your complaints, criticisms and frustrations — and bring your focus to whatever positives there are around you. Don't expect it to turn around overnight. Keep it up, and commit to it.

In so doing, you release your resistance to better circumstances that are waiting in the wings to become your new reality.

As a path of consciousness, the Law of Attraction reminds you to keep the faith in the face of adversity. It reminds you to stay positive, because what you embody now will have its time too. It reminds you that you are not a victim of your circumstances (even though it sometimes feels like you are.) If you were a victim, you'd have no choices. But each moment you have the choice to bring forth whatever attitude you want to bring. So notice when you're going it alone and getting bogged down in trying to solve the problems of your life. Then hand it over to the Universe and open your heart to the guidance it gives.

To harness the power of the Law of Attraction, you make it a daily practice and let it shift your reality into a dance of co-creation. You don't have to do more; just dream better. You don't have to work harder; just love more. Bring excitement, celebration, appreciation and joy into your activities. Raise your spirits, raise your thoughts, and raise your awareness of the infinite creation around you. Radiate love and gratitude towards everything you interact with, and it will come back to you profoundly. To master the Law of Attraction, hand over the reins to the Powers that Be and become a willing vessel to attract and actualize the highest good for yourself and for all those whose lives you touch.

Now that's something to celebrate!

DON'T STOP NOW

YOUR FREE 5 DAY SAMPLE of "30 DAY LAW OF ATTRACTION JOURNAL" - JUST A FEW PAGES AHEAD

BEFORE MOVING ON, WE WANT TO THANK YOU SINCERLEY FOR READ OUR BOOK.

WE GENUINLEY LOVE WHAT WE DO! OUR GOAL IS TO CONSTANTLY EXPAND THE WORLDS MIND IN ALL THINGS TRANSFORMATION.

PLEASE GO BACK AND GIVE US A GREAT REVIEW ON AMAZON SO WE CAN CONTINUE ON SHARING OUR MESSAGE. THANK YOU!

FREE BONUS HERE

When I first committed to understanding the Law of Attraction, I used this exact journal daily… and it *TRANSFORMED MY LIFE.*

As a way to *thank you* for investing in yourself with this book…

I pass my 30 Day Law of Attraction Journal on to you… for *FREE.*

I do ask just one thing…Use it.

DOWNLOAD HERE FOR FREE - 30 Day Journal: http://secretsofthelaw.com/

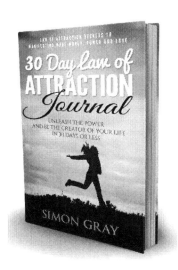

MY LAW OF ATTRACTION JOURNAL

Now that you have in your hands all the pieces of the puzzle to work with the Law of Attraction and magnetize your heart's desires, you're ready to get started making miracles! Simply understanding these profound principles theoretically isn't enough; change happens when you make them an integral part of your life, your thoughts, your responses to experiences, and your whole way of being in the world. Making real and lasting change in your life requires repetition, focus, and commitment.

To help you really bring it all home, we give you your own *Law of Attraction Journal*, designed to inspire you and provide a repetitive platform and a fun, focalizing tool to attract what you want in your life. Use your *Journal* to keep a record of what you're discovering and how your awareness is growing as you work. Write down your reflections and what you notice coming back to you in your life. Acknowledge your achievements and forgive your imperfections. And record every miracle that comes your way!

Your Journal is your 30-day jumpstart to working powerfully with the Law of Attraction. It includes 30 pages, one for each day, for you to write down:

• What you're focusing on to attract into your life

You might focus on one thing for the whole 30 days. Whatever you choose, writing it at the top of the page will keep you focused

• What exercises you did that day

Keep a record of what you're doing. It'll keep you on track and boost your confidence too.

• Your accomplishments, discoveries, healings

Write down every little thing you did well. Mention the times when you let go of negativity or chose to resonate with joy or other positive feelings. Record how you're feeling and if the world is responding to you any differently.

• What you're grateful for

Write down at least twenty things you're grateful for. Really. If it's hard for you to come up with twenty things, then it's especially important that you do this! A smile on someone's face. Your comfortable mattress. The TV that lasted far longer than it should have. The meal someone cooked for you. There is so much to be grateful for; take a moment to acknowledge them. (You can repeat one day to the next if you need to.)

• The day's signs, messages and miracles

Write down any results you're experiencing, the big ones and the small ones! Note down surprises and unexpected gifts, signs and encouragements along the way.

Before you start using your *Journal*, make a list of all of the techniques and exercises in this book that call to you. Then come up with a ballpark figure of the amount of time you think you need or want to devote to each exercise. Finally, decide how frequently you are choosing to do your Law of Attraction work. Perhaps you only have 15 minutes in the morning or maybe a half hour at night. Maybe you can fit in a whole hour at lunchtime. Or maybe your life is full to the brim and you can only realistically give yourself a half hour, three times a week. Come up with an interval of time that feels comfortable to you; if you are unrealistic and you overcommit, you're just setting yourself up for failure. That won't serve you. Instead, check with your logical side and your feeling side and find the happy medium. Make a commitment to yourself for whatever frequency and length of time that feels good to you.

Working with your *Journal* every day is a gift you give yourself, after all. It is an act of deep love to set your intentions, arrange your life, and make the commitment to bring yourself what you most want in your life. It will focalize your creative thoughts, open your mind and heart to virtually unlimited possibilities, and help you realize your most fervent dreams and your deepest desires. Congratulations in advance for all of your successes and for your dreams come true!

Day 1   Date: _____

The only limit to your impact is your imagination and commitment.

—Tony Robbins

What I'm choosing to attract in my life:

_____

_____

_____

_____

Today's exercises:

_____

_____

_____

_____

Accomplishments, discoveries, healings:

_____

_____

_____

_____

What and who I'm grateful for:

_____

_____

_____

_____

Today's signs, messages and miracles:

_____

_____

_____

_____

Day 2   Date: _____

Day 2: Discontent, blaming, complaining, self-pity cannot serve as a foundation for a good future, no matter how much effort you make.

—Eckhart Tolle

What I'm choosing to attract in my life:

_____

_____

_____

_____

Today's exercises:

_____

_____

_____

_____

Accomplishments, discoveries, healings:

_____

_____

_____

_____

What and who I'm grateful for:

_____

_____

_____

_____

Today's signs, messages and miracles:

_____

_____

_____

_____

Day 3   Date: _____

Day 3: The power for creating a better future is contained in the present moment: You create a good future by creating a good present.

—Eckhart Tolle

What I'm choosing to attract in my life:

_____

_____

_____

_____

Today's exercises:

_____

_____

_____

_____

Accomplishments, discoveries, healings:

_____

_____

_____

_____

What and who I'm grateful for:

_____

_____

_____

_____

Today's signs, messages and miracles:

_____

_____

_____

_____

Day 4   Date: _____

Day 4: Spread love everywhere you go. Let no one ever come to you without leaving happier.

—Mother Teresa

What I'm choosing to attract in my life:

_____

_____

_____

_____

Today's exercises:

_____

_____

_____

_____

Accomplishments, discoveries, healings:

_____

_____

_____

_____

What and who I'm grateful for:

_____

_____

_____

_____

Today's signs, messages and miracles:

_____

_____

_____

_____

Day 5   Date: _____

Day 5: Our deepest fear is not that we are inadequate. Our deepest fear is that we are powerful beyond measure. It is our Light, not our Darkness, that most frightens us.

—Marianne Williamson

What I'm choosing to attract in my life:

_____

_____

_____

_____

Today's exercises:

_____

_____

_____

_____

Accomplishments, discoveries, healings:

_____

_____

_____

_____

What and who I'm grateful for:

_____

_____

_____

_____

Today's signs, messages and miracles:

_____

_____

_____

_____

FREE BONUS HERE

When I first committed to understanding the Law of Attraction, I used this exact journal daily... and it *TRANSFORMED MY LIFE.*

As a way to *thank you* for investing in yourself with this book...

I pass my 30 Day Law of Attraction Journal on to you... for *FREE.*

I do ask just one thing...Use it.

DOWNLOAD HERE FOR FREE - 30 Day

Journal: http://secretsofthelaw.com/

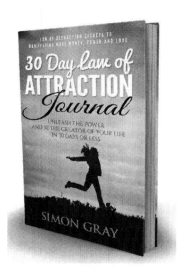

23955103R00051

Printed in Poland
by Amazon Fulfillment
Poland Sp. z o.o., Wrocław